ANIMAL ABCS

ROSE O'KEEFE
John K. Bender & Friends

ANIMAL ABCS

This is a work of fiction. Names, characters, places, and incidents either are the product of the author's imagination or are used fictitiously. Any resemblance to actual persons, living or dead, events, or locales is entirely coincidental.

Copyright © 2021 by Rose O'Keefe

All rights reserved. No part of this book may be reproduced or used in any manner without written permission of the copyright owner except for the use of quotations in a book review. For more information, address: billelliot@elliot.com.

First paperback edition October 2021

Book design by Stephen Huffaker
Illustration by John K. Bender

978-1-7377803-1-1
978-1-7377803-0-4

www.rokeefehistory.com

This book is dedicated to anyone who was bored and lonely during the pandemic.

Special thanks to John Bender and my writing friends.

Introduction

Animal ABCs *is a word game for people who enjoy a search that gets harder as it goes along; who enjoy unusual words and consider a dictionary one of their favorite books or research tools. There is a pattern, that we will leave to the curious reader to unlock on their own.*

Ant.
Abe and Ange arrive at the airport.
Abs, ace, air, arm, auk.

Bat, Ant.
Brynn and Burk bike to the bodega and the beach.
Bake, best, bird, book, buy.

Crow, Ant, Bat.
Carl and Cate count cookies.
Ceci and Cedric search for cereal in the center of the cupboard.
Chaz and Cher change chairs.
Cat, chew, circle, cool, cut, cry.

Dove, Ant, Bat, Crow.
Deb and her dad Djed do daily deliveries on damp and dry days.
Dark, deck, dive, dog, dug, dry.

Eel, Ant, Bat, Crow, Dove.
Emma and Evan enjoy the escalator.
Ear, eek! eight, eon, eugh.

Fox, Ant, Bat, Crow, Dove, Eel.
Fran and Frank feel fabulous in fuzzy fur outfits.
Face, feel, fish, found, fruit.

Goat, Ant, Bat, Crow, Dove, Eel, Fox.
Glynis and Greg grow green beans in the garden.
Gerome and Ginette enjoy ginger ale.
Gate, gem, gild, got, gum.

Hen, Ant, Bat, Crow, Dove, Eel, Fox, Goat.
Hy and Herm have a huge hug from a superhero.
Hat, health, hike, home, hunt.

Ide, Ant, Bat, Crow, Dove, Eel, Fox, Goat, Hen.
Irv and Izz imagine icebergs from their home in India.
Ian, I, ink, ion, it.

Jay, Ant, Bat, Crow, Dove, Eel, Fox, Goat, Hen, Ide.
Jake and Joan jump into a jeep for a jamboree.
Jade, jet, jinx, jot, jump.

Kite, Ant, Bat, Crow, Dove, Eel, Fox, Goat, Hen, Ide, Jay.
Kris and Kyle keep their kitten in the kitchen.
Kale, kept, kin, knock, kvetch.

Lynx, Ant, Bat, Crow, Dove, Eel, Fox, Goat, Hen, Ide, Jay, Kite.
Lars and Lynn like to laugh on a lovely day.
Lab, leaf, light, loud, lunch.

**Midge, Ant, Bat, Crow, Dove, Eel,
Fox, Goat, Hen, Ide, Jay, Kite, Lynx.**
Merle and Mike must meet their mentor in minutes.
Map, meek, mist, more, mulch.

**Naja, Aardvark, Badger, Cougar,
Dingo, Egret, Ferret, Greenfinch,
Heron, Ibis, Jackal, Kagu, Lizard,
Monkey.**
Nathan and Nicole nap before New Year's noshing.
Native, needle, nickel, nosey, numbers.

**Orca, Aardvark, Badger, Cougar,
Dingo, Egret, Ferret, Greenfinch,
Heron, Ibis, Jackal, Kagu, Lizard,
Monkey, Naja.**
Oscar and Olive go out for onion bagels.
Oakling, open, oily, oopsie, outlet.

**Parrot, Aardvark, Badger, Cougar,
Dingo, Egret, Ferret, Greenfinch,
Heron, Ibis, Jackal, Kagu, Lizard,
Monkey, Naja, Orca.**
Patrick and Penny play ping pong and pickle ball.
Philip and Phila phone for phat tai.
Paper, peanuts, picnic, phony, purchase.

**Quetzal, Aardvark, Badger, Cougar,
Dingo, Egret, Ferret, Greenfinch,
Heron, Ibis, Jackal, Kagu, Lizard,
Monkey, Naja, Orca, Parrot.**
Queenie and Quincy quit quibbling.
Qatar, question, quiet, quota, quu.

**Raven, Aardvark, Badger, Cougar, Dingo,
Egret, Ferret, Greenfinch, Heron, Ibis,
Jackal, Kagu, Lizard, Monkey, Naja,
Orca, Parrot, Quetzal.**
Rhoda and Ringo roast red peppers for the rice 'n beans.
Rainbow, request, ribbon, roaster, rumple.

Skua, Aardvark, Badger, Cougar,
Dingo, Egret, Ferret, Greenfinch,
Heron, Ibis, Jackal, Kagu, Lizard,
Monkey, Naja, Orca, Penguin,
Quetzal, Raven.
Savvi and Stella can't sit still.
Shannon and Shalhoob share shawarmas.
Sandy, secret, scissors, shampoo, sunrise.

Tigress, Aardvark, Badger, Cougar,
Dingo, Egret, Ferret, Greenfinch,
Heron, Ibis, Jackal, Kagu, Lizard,
Monkey, Naja, Orca, Penguin,
Quetzal, Raven, Skua.
Tremell and Tammi travel by train to Tibet.
Theo and Thelma think about thunder storms.
Take-out, theme park, tiptoe, towel, turnstile.

Urchin, Aardvark, Badger,
Cougar, Dingo, Egret, Ferret,
Greenfinch, Heron, Ibis, Jackal,
Kagu, Lizard, Monkey, Naja,
Orca, Penguin, Quetzal, Raven,
Skua, Tigress.
Umbert and Ursa understand how to use an umbrella.
Udal, under, unite, unlock, utter.

**Vulture, Aardvark, Badger,
Cougar, Dingo, Egret, Ferret,
Greenfinch, Heron, Ibis, Jackal,
Kagu, Lizard, Monkey, Naja,
Orca, Penguin, Quetzal, Raven,
Skua, Tigress, Urchin.**
Vinnie and Vivi view vacation videos.
Vacate, very, visor, voices, vulpine.

Walrus, Aardvark, Badger,
Cougar, Dingo, Egret, Ferret,
Greenfinch, Heron, Ibis, Jackal,
Kagu, Lizard, Monkey, Naja,
Orca, Penguin, Quetzal, Raven,
Skua, Tigress, Urchin, Vulture.
Wanda walks with Wesley in his wheelchair at the wedding.
Walker, wheelie, writing, wormhole, wouldn't.

Xema, Aardvark, Badger, Cougar,
Dingo, Egret, Ferret, Greenfinch,
Heron, Ibis, Jackal, Kagu, Lizard,
Monkey, Naja, Orca, Penguin,
Quetzal, Raven, Skua, Tigress,
Urchin, Vulture, Walrus.
Xander and Xavier exit excitedly.
Xanthin, xebec, xylem, xyloid, xyphoid.

Yakin, Aardvark, Badger, Cougar, Dingo, Egret, Ferret, Greenfinch, Heron, Ibis, Jackal, Kagu, Lizard, Monkey, Naja, Orca, Penguin, Quetzal, Raven, Skua, Tigress, Urchin, Vulture, Walrus, Xema.
Yuval and Yvonne used yoyos yesterday.
Yaffle, yellow, yipping, yogurt, yummy.

Zebra, Aardvark, Badger, Cougar, Dingo, Egret, Ferret, Greenfinch, Heron, Ibis, Jackal, Kagu, Lizard, Monkey, Naja, Orca, Penguin, Quetzal, Raven, Skua, Tigress, Urchin, Vulture, Walrus, Xema, Yakin.
Zadik and Zoe zoom to the zoo.
Zigzag, zero, ZIP code, zodiac, Zumba.

Cheat Sheet

This little project started during a heat wave when I was on vacation. It was too hot to go outdoors and I'd finished all the books I'd brought with me. I fiddled online with an ABC booklet. It started with words of one syllable and after many versions had half the alphabet that way and the rest with two syllables. Examples follow a pattern for the most part. There are a few that don't fit perfectly – are they bloopers or good enough?

Notes or Doodles

Notes or Doodles

Notes or Doodles

www.ingramcontent.com/pod-product-compliance
Lightning Source LLC
Chambersburg PA
CBHW072210100526
44589CB00015B/2469